Ants

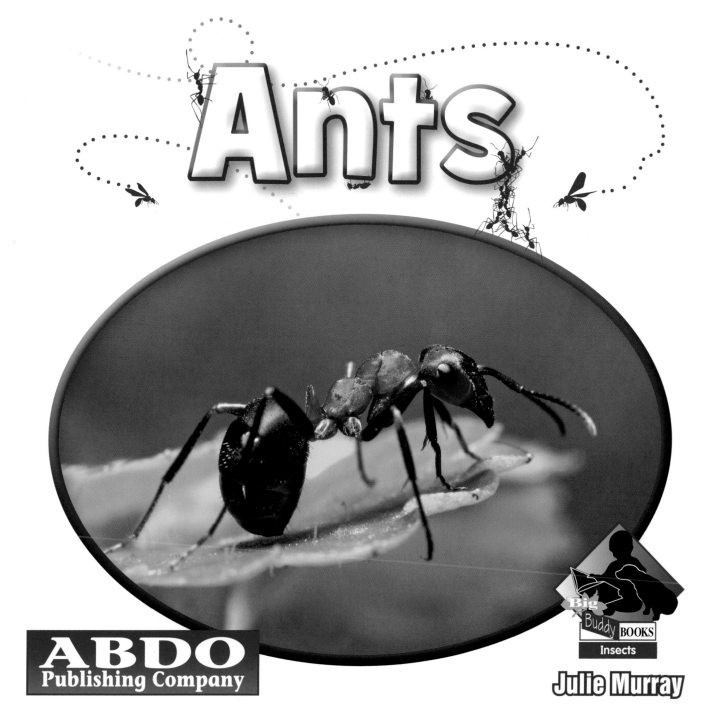

ABDO Publishing Company

Big Buddy BOOKS
Insects

Julie Murray

VISIT US AT
www.abdopublishing.com

Published by ABDO Publishing Company, 8000 West 78th Street, Edina, Minnesota 55439.

Copyright © 2011 by Abdo Consulting Group, Inc. International copyrights reserved in all countries. No part of this book may be reproduced in any form without written permission from the publisher. Big Buddy Books™ is a trademark and logo of ABDO Publishing Company.

Printed in the United States of America, North Mankato, Minnesota.
042010
092010

 PRINTED ON RECYCLED PAPER

Coordinating Series Editor: Rochelle Baltzer
Editor: Sarah Tieck
Contributing Editors: Heidi M.D. Elston, Megan M. Gunderson, BreAnn Rumsch, Marcia Zappa
Graphic Design: Maria Hosley
Cover Photograph: *Shutterstock*: Stana.
Interior Photographs/Illustrations: *AnimalsAnimals - Earth Scenes*: Michael Dick (p. 12); *iStockphoto*: ©iStockphoto.com/Cabezonication (p. 11), ©iStockphoto.com/Kaphoto (p. 7); *Minden Pictures*: Satoshi Kuribayashi/Nature Production (p. 17), Mark Moffett (p. 13), Piotr Naskrecki (p. 23); *Peter Arnold, Inc.*: ©Biosphoto/Koenig Christian (p. 19), ©Biosphoto/Dominique Delfino (p. 25), ©Biosphoto/Olivier Patrice (p. 30), ©Biosphoto/Crocetta Tony (p. 25), Doug Cheeseman (p. 23), Michael J. Doolittle (p. 15), Muehimann, K. (p. 29), WILDLIFE (p. 12); *Photo Researchers, Inc.*: James H. Robinson (p. 27), Sinclair Stammers (p. 20), Francesco Tomasinelli (pp. 13, 21, 30); *Shutterstock*: Eric Isselée (p. 5), Dr. Morley Read (p. 9), Jens Stolt (p. 5).

Library of Congress Cataloging-in-Publication Data

Murray, Julie, 1969-
  Ants / Julie Murray.
    p. cm. -- (Insects)
  ISBN 978-1-61613-481-5
  1. Ants--Juvenile literature. I. Title. II. Series: Murray, Julie, 1969- Insects.
  QL568.F7M87 2010
  595.79'6--dc22
                              2010000784

Contents

Insect World

Millions of insects live throughout the world. They are found on the ground, in the air, and in the water. Some have existed since before dinosaurs!

Ants are one type of insect. They live in many different places including jungles, woods, and fields. You may even find ants in a city or in your backyard.

Bug Bite!

Ants are close relatives of sawflies, wasps, and bees.

Ants are usually black, brown, red, or yellow in color.

An Ant's Body

Like all insects, an ant has three main body parts. These are the head, the thorax, and the abdomen.
An ant's head has eyes, antennae, and a mouth. Its mouth has special parts called mandibles. Ants use their mandibles to carry objects or to fight.

Bug Bite!

Most ants are less than one inch (2.5 cm) long.

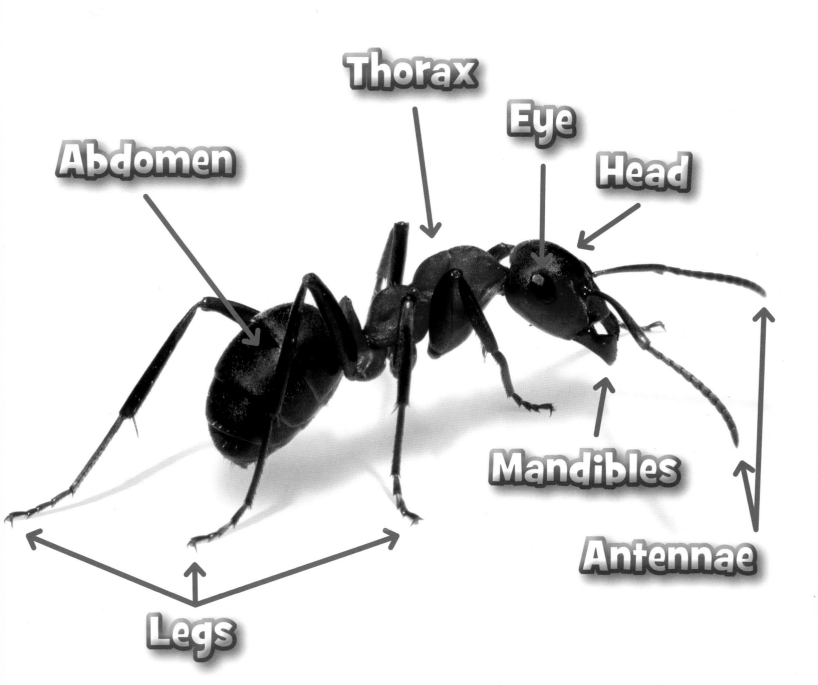

Thorax

Eye

Head

Abdomen

Mandibles

Antennae

Legs

An ant's legs connect to its **thorax**. If an ant has wings, they also connect to the thorax.

Important **organs** are inside the **abdomen**. And, some ants have a stinger on the end of the abdomen.

Instead of bones, an ant has an exoskeleton. The exoskeleton supports its weight and **protects** its organs. It is lightweight. So, an ant can use most of its **muscle** power to carry heavy loads.

Leaf-cutter ants cut and carry big pieces of leaves with their strong mandibles.

An Ant's Life

Ants live and work together as a colony. Colonies include workers, males, and at least one queen.

Together, colony members build nests and hunt, gather, or grow food. They also feed and **protect** their colony's young.

Bug Bite! Ants smell each other with their antennae when they meet!

Bug Bite!

Scientists have found more than 10,000 different types of ants!

Colonies can be large or small. Some of the largest colonies include thousands of ants!

In the Nest

Tunnels and rooms (*above*) are inside ant nests (*right*).

Most ant colonies live in nests. Some ant nests look like dirt mounds. Other nests may be in rotted logs, hidden underground, or high in treetops. Adult ants build and care for the nests.

Weaver ants use leaves to build their nests. To do this, they pull leaves together with their strong mandibles.

Bug Bite! Weaver ant larvae make sticky silk. These ants use it to glue leaves together for their nest.

Life Begins

An ant goes through four different life stages. These stages are egg, larva, pupa, and adult.

All ants begin life as eggs. Queen ants lay the eggs. In new colonies, queens care for their young. As the colony grows, workers take over this job.

Life Cycle of a Bullet Ant

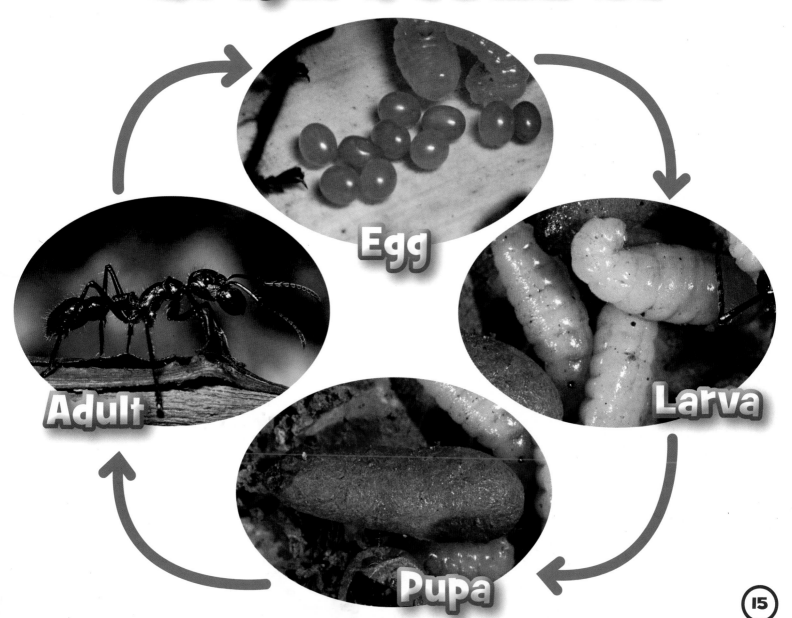

Egg

Larva

Pupa

Adult

After a few days, the eggs **hatch**. Wormlike larvae come out. The larvae **shed** their skin several times as they grow.

When they have grown enough, larvae become pupae. Some larvae spin cocoons. Others grow skin. During this stage, a pupa changes into an adult. In time, an adult ant crawls out of its cocoon or sheds its skin.

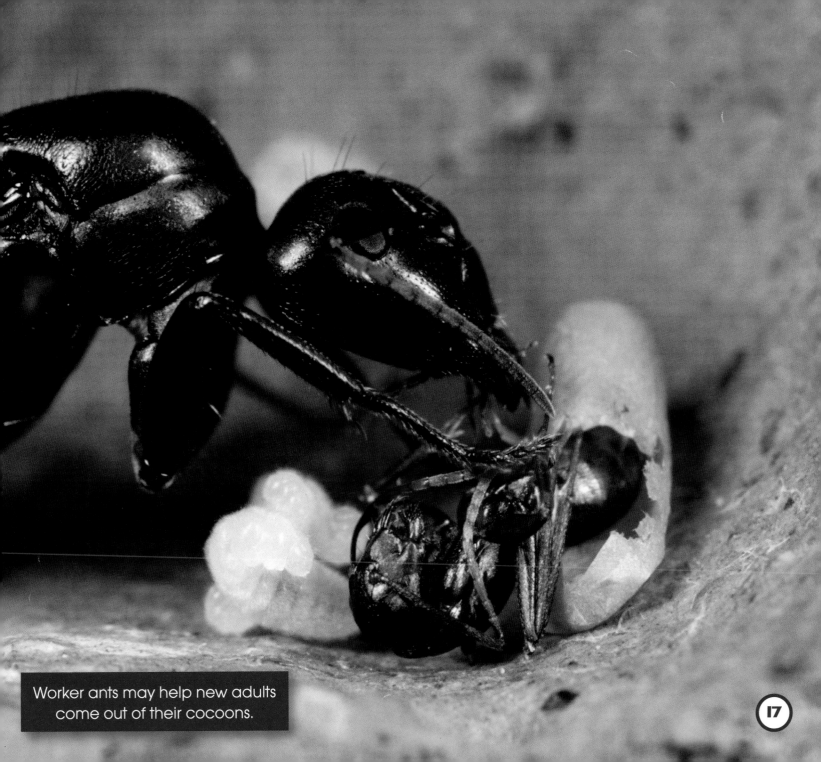

Worker ants may help new adults come out of their cocoons.

Teamwork

Each adult ant in a colony has a job to do. By working together, they are able to survive.

Young queen ants **mate** with males. After mating, queens start a new colony or join an existing one. The queens spend their lives laying eggs.

Bug Bite!

Most young queens and male ants have wings. This allows them to leave the nest to mate.

Some types of queen ants lay thousands of eggs during their lifetime!

Army ants move from place to place. They don't have nests like other types of ants. Workers carry their young as the colony moves.

Most of the ants in a nest are workers. Workers are females. They do many jobs. They build nests and farm, gather, or hunt food. Workers also feed and clean young ants and the queen.

A soldier army ant's body is made for fighting.

The largest workers serve as soldiers. They **protect** the nest. For example, soldiers attack enemies that try to enter the nest.

Good Eats

Ants spend a lot of time gathering or making food. They eat many things including seeds, honeydew, and other insects.

Many ants have a special way of telling each other where food is. When an ant searches for food, it marks a trail with **chemicals**. Then, other ants can follow the trail to find the food.

Bug Bite!

Honeydew is a sugary liquid made by other insects.

Leaf-cutter ants use leaf pieces to create a garden in their underground nest. They grow a special food in their garden.

Army ants travel in long lines. They hunt as a group.

23

Danger Zone

Ants face many predators. These include anteaters, birds, and certain insects.

Ants have several ways to **protect** themselves. Some bite, sting, or shoot out harmful **chemicals**. Others run away or play dead.

Bug Bite!

Some ants let out a chemical to protect themselves. Yet, certain birds find this defense helpful! They put these ants in their feathers. This may help get rid of insect pests.

Anteaters use their long tongues to catch ants.

Some birds snack on ants. They may grab a mouthful of them from their nest!

The colors of some ants **protect** them. In the insect world, bold or bright colors often mean danger. So, most predators stay away from red, black, or yellow ants. These ants are likely poisonous or can sting.

Fire ants are often red. Their color is a warning. They are known to sting.

Special Insects

Ants do important work in nature. When they eat other insects, they **protect** plants. And, their underground homes keep soil healthy. This helps farmers and gardeners.

Ants may sneak into people's homes and food. So, they are sometimes considered pests. But, ants help keep the natural world in balance. This protects life on Earth.

Red wood ants eat insect pests such as caterpillars. This helps protect crops.

Bug-O-Rama

What do male ants do?

Their only job is to **mate** with young queen ants. This is very important to the colony. It makes sure the colony carries on.

Can ants attack people?

Most ants are harmless. But some, such as fire ants, can sting people. This can cause the skin to burn and a sore to appear. A person may need a doctor's help.

Do ants live everywhere?

Almost! They don't live in very cold places, such as Antarctica.

Important Words

abdomen (AB-duh-muhn) the back part of an insect's body.

chemical (KEH-mih-kuhl) a substance that can cause reactions and changes.

hatch to be born from an egg.

mate to join as a couple in order to reproduce, or have babies.

muscle (MUH-suhl) body tissue, or layers of cells, that help the body move.

organ a body part that does a special job. The heart and the lungs are organs.

protect (pruh-TEHKT) to guard against harm or danger.

shed to cast aside or lose as part of a natural process of life.

thorax the middle part of an insect's body.

Web Sites

To learn more about ants, visit ABDO Publishing Company online. Web sites about ants are featured on our Book Links page. These links are routinely monitored and updated to provide the most current information available.

www.abdopublishing.com

Index